I0492159

TOP TWENTY WAYS TO USE DRONES
FOR VISUAL INSPECTIONS BY
FAA-LICENSED DRONE SERVICE
PROVIDER NATHAN W. ROSEMAN
OF JAMESTOWN, NEW YORK

For more information, please contact Nathan W. Roseman at (716) 499-0461

TOP TWENTY WAYS TO USE DRONES FOR VISUAL INSPECTIONS BY FAA-LICENSED DRONE SERVICE PROVIDER NATHAN W. ROSEMAN OF JAMESTOWN, NEW YORK

These days, drone inspections are being performed in almost every industry that requires visual inspections as part of its maintenance procedures.

By using a drone to <u>collect visual data</u> on the condition of an asset, drone inspections help inspectors avoid having to place themselves in dangerous situations.

Instead of climbing several stories in the air on a tower to take a close look at a guy-wire, or on scaffolding within a <u>boiler</u> to look at a weld, an inspector can send a drone instead.

In this comprehensive guide to drone inspections we're going to walk through the requirements of a typical inspection, how drones fit into the process, the benefits of using drones for inspections, and then take a look at all the different industries currently using drones for their inspection-related needs.

In case you'd like to jump around we've created this table of contents:

- <u>What Is a Visual Inspection and Why Is It Important</u>
- <u>The Benefits of Drone Inspections Inspection</u>
- <u>Inspection Standards and Formal Inspection Bodies</u>
- <u>Drone Inspections by Industry</u>

What Is a Visual Inspection and Why Is It Important?

A visual inspection is exactly what it sounds like: a careful, thorough review with the naked eye of every single part of an asset.

In many instances, a drone inspection will be a visual inspection, with the drone's camera acting as the inspector's eyes. Using a drone, visual data is collected and then reviewed in detail later by the inspector (some review is done on the spot, too, but the thorough inspection after data is collected represents the bulk of the visual inspection work).

When inspecting a cell phone tower, for example, an inspector will climb the entire tower looking for areas that might need maintenance. For indoor inspections, such as those performed inside boilers or pressure vessels, inspectors must build scaffolding so they can climb up the sides of the boiler, visually reviewing every square inch as they go.

Visual inspections are critical to ensuring the proper maintenance of a company's assets. After all, it's a lot easier, not to mention cheaper, to replace a few rivets on a tower than to build a brand new tower. But visual inspections aren't just about saving money. They're also about saving lives.

In the case of a pressure vessel, a visual inspection can help uncover potential problems that could lead to life-threatening hazards if not properly addressed. If the vessel isn't properly maintained it could explode, endangering the lives of everyone in the area.

NOT ALL DRONE INSPECTIONS ARE VISUAL

While it's true that most drone inspections are visual inspections, with the drone simply taking the place of the inspector's eyes, drones can also

Page 3

be equipped with special sensors that allow them to perform other kinds of inspections. Basically, any kind of sensor that can fit on a UAV can be used for an inspection.

For example, in agriculture drones are being outfitted with multispectral sensors so that farmers can record images of crops in distinct spectral bands. And in HVAC inspections, some inspectors are putting a thermal camera on their drone to identify where heat is leaking out of a building.

WHERE INSPECTIONS FIT IN THE MAINTENANCE PROCESS

Before we dive into specific ways drones are being used in visual inspections throughout various industries, let's first review how inspections fit into the overall maintenance process.

When caring for any kind of asset, whether it's a pressure vessel or a power line, the same general procedure is followed: first you inspect, then you repair (assuming the inspection reveals that repairs are needed).

Drones help with the first step—inspections. By sending a UAV into a situation that would be dangerous for a person, like into a chimney or up a cell phone tower, inspectors are able to collect visual data about the condition of an asset without having to expose themselves to potential harm.

In this comprehensive guide to drone inspections we're going to walk through the requirements of a typical inspection, how drones fit into the process, the benefits of using drones for inspections, and then take a look at all the different industries currently using drones for their inspection-related needs.

FOR MORE INFORMATION, PLEASE CONTACT NATHAN W. ROSEMAN AT (716) 499-0461

The Benefits of Drone Inspections

We've already discussed the fact that drone inspections can help keep inspectors safe by removing the need for them to enter potentially dangerous scenarios, like climbing towers or high scaffolding. But drone inspections can also save companies a lot of money.

How?

First, recall that inspections are just the first step of the maintenance process. The second step is the actual maintenance.

But inspections often don't find anything that needs to be fixed—it's not uncommon for only 10-20% of inspections to actually find a problem that requires fixing.

In those instances that do require maintenance, a person will have to be physically present to fix the problem. (We haven't built drones that can turn a screwdriver or perform the complicated operations needed for maintenance—not yet, anyway.)

But 80-90% of the time the inspection does not uncover work that needs to be performed, which means that a drone could potentially be used for the full maintenance process 80-90% of the time.

Why is this important?

Because building scaffolding to allow a person to perform a manual inspection is incredibly expensive. By only building scaffolding when actual maintenance is required, companies can reduce their corresponding maintenance expenses by up to 80-90%, which could mean a savings of tens of thousands, and in some cases even hundreds of thousands of dollars.

Building scaffolding also takes time. When conducting inspections manually, often a full day is required for constructing scaffolding and then a full day for taking it down, which means dozens of hours of downtime for the asset being inspected. In many cases, that downtime equals a significant loss of potential revenue for the company.

Finally, whether an inspection requires scaffolding or not, reducing the time an inspector has to be put into a dangerous situation by 80-90% represents a huge potential saving in liability insurance costs.

Now that we've provided an overview of how drone inspections can help with both safety and savings, let's list out their primary benefits:

- **Reduced risk**. Inspector no longer has to be put into potentially dangerous situations.

- **Savings—temporary structures**. Savings as a result of not needing to build scaffolding or other temporary, one-use infrastructure to support a manual inspection (as applicable—not all inspection scenarios require scaffolding).

- **Savings—downtime**. For assets like nuclear power plants or pressure vessels, which need to be shut off before an inspection can be performed, every second of downtime means a loss of revenue. Using a drone to make turnarounds more efficient can mean big savings for companies that use these assets in their operations.

- **Savings—liability insurance**. By significantly reducing the amount of time personnel is placed in dangerous situations companies can reduce their corresponding insurance costs.

- **Increased safety through increased inspections**. Given the relatively low cost of drone inspections, many companies are using them to perform inspections more regularly, which means that potential problems can be surfaced and addressed more quickly.

- **Better records**. Drone data represents a meticulous record of the condition of an asset over time. By archiving visual data, companies have a digital footprint of the asset's life history that can be accessed at any time.

Read this article from Bloomberg News to learn more about how drones help keep people out of danger.

Inspection Standards and Formal Inspection Bodies

Most industries that have assets that could be dangerous if not properly maintained don't just do inspections because they're a good idea. They also do them because they're required by law.

INSPECTION STANDARDS

For the inspections of assets that could explode or present other safety hazards if not properly maintained—we're talking about pressure vessels, boilers, and nuclear power plants, as well as other containers that hold chemicals or volatile substances—the laws in most countries require specific standards be followed when inspecting them.

These inspection standards are usually the same and are created by associations with a specific focus on a given industry.

For example, inspections in Energy usually adhere to the API standards (American Petroleum Institute). ASME (American Society of

Mechanical Engineers), on the other hand, is a standards organization that creates codes specifically for the design, construction, and inspection of boilers and pressure vessels.

But these are just a few examples. There are several organizations like API and ASME devoted to creating standards and training materials for various industries in which inspections are performed, and their standards are mandated by law in most countries throughout the world.

FORMAL INSPECTION BODIES

For the inspection of dangerous assets, the law in most countries requires not only that certain standards be followed but also that a representative from a formal inspection body is present for the inspection.

A formal inspection body is a private company that provides trained, certified inspectors to authenticate inspections as having been done following the mandated standards. These inspectors usually go through rigorous training and testing provided by and/or certified by a given standards organization before earning a certificate that grants them permission to authenticate inspections of a given type.

While a standards-making association like API may have fairly general requirements for a given inspection, a formal inspection body will often have more detailed standards for their inspectors, which they have created themselves.

"Every inspection has its own unique challenges, which means that certified API inspectors must be highly trained in order to make their own judgment calls in the field. If an API-certified inspector makes a decision on RVI [Remote Visual Inspection] or any other tool during an

FOR MORE INFORMATION, PLEASE CONTACT NATHAN W. ROSEMAN AT (716) 499-0461

inspection, this decision is drawing on a high level of knowledge and experience."

When overseeing an inspection, it is ultimately up to the representatives of the formal inspection body to draw on their training and decide if the proposed tool—say, a camera attached to a drone—can take the place of the naked eye, as well as making other determinations about whether the inspection protocol is being followed properly.

DO FORMAL INSPECTION BODIES ALLOW DRONES TO BE USED IN INSPECTIONS?

Most standards organizations are solution- and company-agnostic, which means they will not specifically endorse a certain tool (for example, a specific type of camera, or drones in general) or a specific company's products for use in inspections.

Instead, both standards organizations and formal inspection bodies rely on each inspector to make an individual judgment call in the field regarding a given tool.

If a representative from a formal inspection body decides that a given tool is collecting adequate visual data—meaning, the same quality of data the inspector could gather with the naked eye—then the representative can designate that tool as a formal inspection tool in that instance.

That being said, because inspections are so crucial to ensuring proper maintenance, many formal inspection bodies have approached drones with some caution.

And with good reason. While a flying camera has the potential to be incredibly helpful for an inspector, most drones are not yet sufficiently developed in terms of accuracy, stability, ease of use, and other key factors to the point where they can completely replace the need for a person to be present.

Drone Inspections by Industry

In the list below, we take a close look at the industries using drone inspections to support their work.

For each industry, we'll describe how drone inspections are being conducted, the benefits drones are providing, the assets drones are being used to inspect, and then list some case studies and resources for further reading.

One thing to note is that inspections conducted by drone can be viewed as falling into two different categories for the purposes of finding the right tool for the job: indoor and outdoor.

Indoor inspections, which are primarily conducted in hard-to-reach, confined spaces will have very different requirements from outdoor inspections in terms of the kinds of drones that can be used and other limiting factors.

List of Industries

- Agriculture
- Chemicals
- Construction
- Infrastructure & Utilities
- Insurance

- <u>Power Generation</u>
- <u>Mining</u>
- <u>Oil & Gas</u>
- <u>Public Safety</u>
- <u>Other Drone Inspection Scenarios</u>

AGRICULTURE DRONE INSPECTIONS

When we think of inspections, we usually imagine industrial assets, like boilers or construction sites, but agricultural drone inspections have been on the rise in the last few years.

Drones are being used in agriculture to provide regular monitoring of crops and livestock, and to create 3D maps of farmland to better understand irrigation conditions and related issues. A drone can provide a regular snapshot of crop conditions in far-flung locations on a large farm, giving the owner quick insights into failing crops so that issues can be addressed before they become worse.

In agriculture, one big benefit of drone inspections is improving crop yield.

Data collected by drone can be used to ensure that crops and soil receive exactly what they need for optimum health and productivity, a practice that has been named *precision agriculture.*

Drones also help farmers save time—lots of it. A drone can provide visual crop data in a quick flight that might otherwise take hours of walking the field. And because data capture is so much quicker by drone, it can be performed more often, thus leading to improved conditions for crops and bigger yields. Drone data can also be used to provide a record of crop health over time, allowing farmers to compare crops from one year to the next or across seasons in order to optimize their yield in various conditions.

ASSETS THAT NEED TO BE INSPECTED/MONITORED

- Crops (monitor health, maturity, damage, and related issues)
- Irrigation conditions
- Overall land conditions
- Soil health
- Livestock

CHEMICAL INDUSTRY DRONE INSPECTIONS

Inspections in the chemical industry are made by any company that makes or requires the storage of chemicals as part of its work, including laboratories.

The need for strict maintenance procedures with these inspections is clear. Any leak as a result of a poorly maintained storage container could result in severe consequences, including problems such as chemicals leaching into the water or earth—scenarios that could pose serious health risks for those in the immediate area.

One major benefit of using drones for inspections in the chemical industry is in reducing exposure to potentially harmful materials. There are also big potential savings from not needing to build scaffolding for inspections, as well as reduced liability concerns.

ASSETS THAT NEED TO BE INSPECTED

- Pipe racks
- Cables
- Conduits
- Fermenter tanks
- Pressure vessels / Storage tanks
- Fiberglass storage tanks
- Suction ducts
- Heat exchangers
- Storage silos and bins

CONSTRUCTION DRONE INSPECTIONS

Construction companies have been using drone inspections for a while now to help gather data quickly on the progress of their projects.

Similar to the benefits drone inspections provide in agriculture, on construction sites the ability to gather aerial data on the status of the entire site quickly and efficiently can be invaluable, and potentially save companies a lot of money.

Here are some of the benefits that construction companies are getting from drones:

- Increased accuracy in reporting
- Increased regularity of reporting
- Improving safety conditions by quickly spotting problems onsite
- Improving efficiency of operations

Drone inspections can also help construction operations with pre-planning, by providing visual data that can be converted into detailed 3D or orthomosaic maps of an area, which can then be used to identify the ideal location for a building.

These maps can be used throughout the life of a construction project to monitor progress, for regular reporting to customers and other stakeholders, and to track and monitor stockpiles of materials onsite.

Of all the benefits of using a drone on a construction site, one of the biggest is in avoiding potential delays. By increasing their regularity of data collection and reporting, construction companies can spot problems well in advance, and avoid running over budget.

ASSETS THAT NEED TO BE INSPECTED

- Land
- Construction site—building itself and surrounding area)
- Stockpiles / aggregates onsite
- Fencing and related safety conditions—to prevent civilians from entering the site
- Safety conditions for the crew—to identify potential problem areas before anyone is injured

INFRASTRUCTURE & UTILITIES DRONE INSPECTIONS

Of all the industry categories on this list, this is one of the broadest. Infrastructure & Utilities includes utility towers, bridges, air transport infrastructure, railways, roads, and more.

Drones are being used in Infrastructure & Utilities for inspections related to regular maintenance, as well as in inspections following disasters like hurricanes and floods, in which the status of existing infrastructure is unknown.

The top benefit of using drone inspections for Infrastructure & Utilities is the ability to gather accurate data quickly and inexpensively. In scenarios that present a potential danger to inspectors, like tower or bridge inspections, an added benefit is the ability to collect key visual data without the need for the inspector to be physically present.

To make this more concrete, visually inspecting a bridge without a drone can require inspectors to rappel into position, sometimes using heavy machinery to support the process, all of which can take several days and be potentially dangerous. Using a drone, inspectors can collect visual data for an entire bridge in just an hour or two, and can do follow-up inspections more regularly because the cost and time required are so much less.

ASSETS THAT NEED TO BE INSPECTED

- Utility towers
- Wind turbines
- Bridges
- Air transport infrastructure, including airstrips and air towers
- Railways
- Roads

Insurance companies have been using drones for roof and other inspections related to insurance adjustments for a while now. In 2019, State Farm was the first company ever to be granted a general waiver to fly Beyond Visual Line of Sight (BVLOS) to conduct inspections for damage assessment related to insurance claims.

The most common inspection use case for drones is inspecting roof damage following a big storm or hurricane. Instead of sending a person physically onto a roof to inspect the damage incurred, a drone inspection can quickly collect visual data on the condition of the roof and record it in a way that can be easily accessed by the insurance company in order to validate insurance claim that's been made.

When a natural disaster hits the need for certified commercial drone pilots in an area can spike, with insurance companies hustling to hire enough pilots to fill their data collection needs.

ASSETS THAT NEED TO BE INSPECTED

- Roofs
- Site (overall condition of the site)
- Buildings and related infrastructure on an insured site
- Car accident scenes
- Farms / crop damage
- Other assets that could be damaged following a natural disaster

Power companies work with several different types of assets that require regular inspections. These include assets used in coal-powered energy production, like boilers and chimneys, as well as those used in greener power sources, like wind turbines and the different components of a hydropower plant.

Power plant inspections are being revolutionized by drone technology. The major benefits to a drone inspection over a traditional inspection, as in many inspection scenarios, are removing the inspector from harm's way and saving money by not having to build scaffolding or other temporary infrastructure to support inspection efforts.

ASSETS THAT NEED TO BE INSPECTED

- Coal-fired boilers
- Nuclear power plants
- Heat recovery steam generators
- Waste incinerators
- Wind turbines
- Hydropower plants
- Solar panels / solar panel farms
- Transformers
- Chimneys / Smokestacks

After a mining operation has removed an ore vein, the large underground hole that remains where the ore was extracted can be incredibly unstable, with material falling from the ceiling and crumbling from the walls.

These areas, called "stopes" in the mining industry, are so dangerous that most countries prohibit mining personnel from entering them by law.

But information on the condition of a stope can be critical for the mining company. Ore might be left behind in the stope which could be reclaimed for profit. Also, mining companies use expensive remote mining equipment that could be destroyed if it's sent into an unstable stope.

Drones present a unique opportunity for the mining industry to be able to gather data on stopes and other areas within mining operations that

FOR MORE INFORMATION, PLEASE CONTACT NATHAN W. ROSEMAN AT (716) 499-0461

would otherwise be impossible to collect. The visual data of excavation sites that drones collect can provide safety assessments previously impossible to conduct, enabling unprecedented access within no-go-zones without exposing workers to underground hazards.

Using new mapping software, aerial data collected by drone can now be leveraged to create 3D maps of stopes, which can then be compared to pre- and post-excavation conditions in order to understand how the area has changed.

The biggest benefit of using drone inspections in mining is in keeping people out of harm's way. Conditions underground can be incredibly unstable and the ability to collect visual data remotely, in a way that keeps mining personnel safe, is a huge value for the entire operation.

Another benefit of using drones in mining is the ability to access information that would otherwise be impossible to collect.

And a third benefit comes in the form of potential savings through identifying uncollected ore, preventing loss of equipment by avoiding having it enter areas where conditions are unstable, and in identifying extra ore that could be extracted from a given area.

This last benefit is worth emphasizing. Remotely operated mining equipment, such as muckers, can be incredibly expensive. Being able to collect visual data on the status of an area before any equipment is sent in can help avoid huge losses from destroyed and damaged equipment.

ASSETS THAT NEED TO BE INSPECTED

- Stopes
- Conveyor belts

FOR MORE INFORMATION, PLEASE CONTACT NATHAN W. ROSEMAN AT (716) 499-0461

- SAG, ball, and grinding mills
- Drop raises
- Stockpile feeders
- Crushers

OIL & GAS DRONE INSPECTIONS

The Oil & Gas industry stores natural gas and gasoline, among other substances, in pressure vessels and storage tanks, which means they must conduct regular inspections of these containers.

Drones are becoming more and more popular for these inspections since they can replace the need to send an inspector into the container. Using a drone for these inspections is beneficial because it removes the need to build scaffolding in order to see the inside of the container close up, thus keeping the inspector from harm's way while also saving money by avoiding the need for building scaffolding for inspection purposes.

Drone inspections aren't just useful for the maintenance of containers that store oil, gasoline, and other materials created in the Oil & Gas industry. They are also important for maintaining the assets used in the production of these materials.

For example, the FCC unit commonly used to convert heavy crude oil components into more valuable fuel products consists of several pipes, cyclones and reactor vessels.

The pipe at the center of this process is the riser, in which the heavy oil is mixed with a powdered catalyst at high temperatures. Inspecting a riser normally requires taking the extreme step of sawing an access hatch in the top of the pipe and lowering an inspector inside on a rope. With a drone, the need to enter the pipe is removed, thus keeping the inspector out of a potentially dangerous situation while also saving time and resources.

ASSETS THAT NEED TO BE INSPECTED

- Chimneys and smokestacks
- Offshore rigs, FPSOS, and drilling ships
- Storage tanks
- Refineries
- Jetties

PUBLIC SAFETY DRONE INSPECTIONS

Drone applications in public safety have grown quickly over the last few years.

Some of the inspection scenarios in which drones are being used in public safety are in live, ongoing events, like locating a missing person in a Search & Rescue operation, capturing aerial intelligence in an active shooter scenario, or getting insights into how a wildfire is spreading.

But public safety personnel also use drones for inspections in situations that aren't active or ongoing, like using aerial data captured by drone to create orthomosaic maps of public places to prepare for a possible active shooter scenario, or using aerial data to investigate a crime scene.

WAYS DRONE INSPECTIONS ARE BEING USED IN PUBLIC SAFETY

- Visual data collection for arson investigations and other forensic data collection scenarios
- Visual data collection of ongoing fires
- Visual data collection of an ongoing crime scene to understand entry and exit points, evaluate hostage scenarios, and help police officers plan next steps
- Accident reconstruction
- Pre-planning for accidents and emergency scenarios, by using aerial data to create maps of highly populated areas like schools and malls that can be referenced in case of a fire, active shooter, or other catastrophic events
- Inspecting public spaces like stadiums and arenas for possible security concerns

OTHER DRONE INSPECTION SCENARIOS

As you can probably tell by now, drone inspections can be conducted almost anywhere an inspection might be needed.

Here are a few more industries currently using drone inspections:

MARITIME DRONE INSPECTIONS

Maritime-related inspections cover inspections of huge container ships used to transport goods, the containers themselves, and conceivably any other inspection need related to shipping by boat.

SEWER & WATER TREATMENT

Underground inspections present several technical difficulties, and inspections related to sewer and water treatment are certainly no inspection.

Drones built specifically for indoor inspections are helping improve the inspection process in this industry by giving inspectors a close view of conditions underground without requiring them to physically enter the area being inspected.

 **Nathan W. Roseman** has had extensive experience in all commercial uses of drone technology over the last ten years.

This includes, but is not limited to, visual inspections of all type of businesses, photography, weddings, roof inspections, building and land surveys, as well as the use of drones to locate and save people lost on hiking trips and who fall overboard while fishing and boating.

The Federal Aviation Administration (FAA) has certified Mr. Roseman to perform these and all other commercial functions for which drone technology is available.

Drones are continually proving to be the most effective method for many industries, helping them better manage risks on the jobsite.
Drones are equipped with extremely efficient and smart payloads, combining outstanding performance with a higher level of safety never before seen in a wide variety of business scenarios.

Nathan W. Roseman takes pride in helping his customers manage risks in confined spaces or hazardous areas much more effectively and efficiently with our aerial data collection methods. His mission is to increase safety in the work field. By using the newest advances in technology, he will complete jobs safer, better and in a more cost-efficient way while providing superior service.

FOR MORE INFORMATION, PLEASE CONTACT NATHAN W. ROSEMAN AT (716) 499-0461

FOR MORE INFORMATION, PLEASE CONTACT NATHAN W. ROSEMAN AT (716) 499-0461